INDIAN
WILDLIFE
THROUGH POEMS

INDIAN WILDLIFE
THROUGH POEMS

H.R. Singh and Neeraj Kumar

PARTRIDGE

ISBN: Softcover   978-1-4828-7331-3
             eBook   978-1-4828-7330-6

To order additional copies of this book, contact
Partridge India
000 800 10062 62
orders.india@partridgepublishing.com

www.partridgepublishing.com/india

CONTENTS

PREFACE

The Indian love for wildlife is widely known. It was from the times of the Emperor Ashoka that wild animals were formally protected in sanctuaries. During his times sanctuaries were known as abhyaranyas. Later, during the days of Mughals, wildlife provided magnificent sport and excitement both for rulers and common man. The traditional ecological knowledge (TEK) and India's wildlife has always been a source of great attraction since ages.

At present the wildlife scenario in India is not very encouraging with man constantly encroaching on the rightful territory of animals. There are centrally sponsored schemes like 'Project Tiger', 'Project Elephant', creation of Protected Areas (PAs) and Wildlife Corridors by the government, still poaching continues unabated. The government remains a witness to the depletion and depredation of nature's richness. It needed Supreme Court's intervention two years ago to issue the guidelines for all tiger reserves to segregate the buffer and core areas. Miffed at the government's laxity, the court had earlier put a blanket ban on wildlife tourism. It resorts to knee-jerk reactions whenever wildlife issues are brought to it by SPCA (Society for Prevention of Cruelty to Animals) or PETA (People for Ethical Treatment of Animals) etc.

The first World Wildlife Day on March 3rd, 2014 is an initiative of the United Nations General Assembly (UNGA) to dedicate a day for imparting wildlife awareness to young minds to understand and appreciate nature and natural resources.

The wildlife in India needs strong attention before it is wiped out completely due to neglect of the people and the government. It was on 3rd March in 1973 that the Convention on International Trade in Endangered Species of Wild Fauna and Flora (CITES) was finalized.

The "*Indian Wildlife through Poems*" has been our dream project. It was on the 3rd March, 2014 that the United Nations observed the First World Wildlife Day when we undertook the writing of this book.

"World Wildlife Day is an opportunity to celebrate the many beautiful and varied forms of wild fauna and flora and to raise awareness of the multitude of benefits that conservation provides to people. At the same time, the Day reminds us of the urgent need to step up the fight against wildlife crime, which has wide-ranging economic, environmental and social impacts.

Wildlife has an intrinsic value and contributes to the ecological, genetic, social, economic, scientific, educational, cultural, recreational and aesthetic aspects of sustainable development and human well-being. 2016 theme is: "*The future of wildlife is in our hands*", with African and Asian elephants being the main focus of global campaigns.

The theme "*The future of wildlife is in our hands*" reinforces the inextricable link between wildlife, people and sustainable development. It is the responsibility of each generation to safeguard wildlife for the following generation. It also imparts the pressing need for national action to ensure the survival in the wild of both charismatic and lesser known species.

With 182 Member States, CITES remains one of the world's most powerful tools for biodiversity conservation through the regulation of trade in wild fauna and flora." (UN Quote from 2016 theme).

This book got completed on 3rd March, 2016; World Wildlife Day; and it is aimed to provide scientific, mythological and ecological insights into the behavioural habits, habitats and charismatic features of Indian Wildlife through poems. It is expected to attract kids, youngsters and wildlife lovers alike in India and across the globe.

We are grateful to Dr. V. K. Bahuguna, IFS and Principal Secretary, Forests, Agriculture and Animal Resources etc. Departments; Government of Tripura, Agartala for writing a wonderful foreword for this book and for his kind words about the book. We are thankful to Dr Saket Badola, IFS, Deputy Director, Corbett Tiger Reserve, India for some of his useful suggestions and his interest in these poems. We also wish to acknowledge the UN for using a quote from '2016 theme of World Wildlife Day' page and a number of other anonymous wildlife biologists whose contributions we could consult as freely available resources from internet.

Last but not the least our sincere thanks are due to Mr Jeric Romano, Ms. Farrina Gailey and Ms. Gemma Ramos, all from Partridge Publishing for their keen interest in publishing this book.

H.R. Singh, Ph.D.
Neeraj Kumar, Ph.D.

3rd March, 2016
World Wildlife Day

Dr. V. K. Bahuguna

PRINCIPAL SECRETARY
Forests, Agriculture and Animal Resources etc. Departments
Government of Tripura
Civil Secretariat, Agartala, P.O. : Kunjaban
West Tripura, Pin Code : 799006
Tele Fax : 0381-2416036 (O), 2414665 (R)
E-mail : bahugunaifs@gmail.com

Foreword

Indian civilization is more than 5000 years old and evolved in the midst of sylvan surroundings full of animals and chirping sounds of birds in thick forests. In this journey the people of this country formed indelible bond with the nature and its different components. The culture, religion, literature, art and music all had been profoundly influenced by wild animals. Be it the Monkey God 'Hanuman', Goddess Durga riding a Tiger or lord Ganesha having Elephant trunk as head or Shiva's neck dangling with a Cobra or lord Vishnu lying on big snake, all are part of our life. It is because of this strong bondage, India has unparallel richness in the world in wild life. For this the credit goes to the people who live in and around the forests for preserving and conserving the rich flora and fauna of the wild. We have Lions, Tigers, Leopards, Elephants, Deer, Antelopes and an array of both herbivores and carnivores thriving in our forests. Our ancestors in 170,000 villages situated in the close vicinity of forests have sacrificed a lot of comforts in their life in bequeathing this rich natural heritage to the present generation of the world. The happiness and colour these wild animals add to our life cannot be measured in any monetary terms. The happiness and joy is the poetry of nature to the mankind.

2.   It is in this regards, the present Book of beautiful poems written by my University Professor Dr. HR Singh, who taught us the nuances of Animal kingdom way back in 1975 and who was my PhD guide as well; is a welcome addition to wild life literature of the country. Very few poems have been written on our wild life particularly on creatures like Honey Bees who are one of the big factors in continuing the natural processes in improving the plant genetics through pollination in our agricultural, horticultural and forestry crops. The emotions are always expressed in a far better manner in poems than in any other form of literatures.

3.   This book will be a milestone in the field of wild life literature and would definitely propel other enthusiasts to write poems on our varied wild life in order to truly celebrate the contributions of wild animals in our life and in maintaining the ecological balance. This book is a fine attempt of mobilization of public opinion in favour of wild life in an era of climate change and concerns for environmental conservation. I would like to congratulate the author for bringing out this wonderful book and thank him for choosing one of his students to write this foreword.

31.03.2014

(Dr. V.K. Bahuguna)

1. The Bumble Bee

An endearing and familiar creature
It flies with a deep buzz
Flower to flower when it flies
Pollination it unknowingly does

Many species trot around the globe
Great Yellow, Jet Black
And others exist
In Himalaya, Cardamom
Is pollinated by them
They are a great
Pollinator of Cucurbits

Male bees fly around
The nest in swarms
And wait for the queen
To come out with warmth

Bumble bees are found more
In cool parts of the globe
In India, they pollinate wild flowers n vegetables
Many a times part of folk lore

In the garden and in the fields
They are loved all through
For animated behaviour
And soft hairy looks

All you can do is sit in your garden
Help all children enjoy humming bees
Tell them, not to be afraid of males
They cannot sting.

2. The Ants

Ants being a social insect
An ant is never alone
After roaming close by
She finds her clone

Pheromones help them
In making a trail
And working like a team
They never take a rest
Quick decisions they take
Have, no time to waste

Their life is a lesson
So often ignored
They never sit 'idle'
They never get 'bored'

For a colony of ants
Nothing seems impossible
Quite attractive is their gait
Their determination is admirable
Bit by bit, they carry food items
Up to twenty times their weight

What an ideal!
They show to the world
Who ignores the tiny ones
For all its tricks
Social insects of repute
Are now studied in robotics

Ants appear programmed
Like robots
Putting up an ideal
Navigation before us
Though marching
Without boots
Ants love tandem-running
And easily follow a trail
Like them, we all love
To return home in a haste

Ants are busiest of all
And often work in peace,
Though gifted with
Weapons of attack and defence
If need be, they can turn
An elephant upside-down
Their formic acid is powerful enough
Turning the enemy red and brown

I still wonder, how this
Ingenious insect was designed?
For they are the tiniest
With most fertile mind.

3. The Butterfly

With a slender body
And club-shaped antennae on head
Chasing a butterfly
Children become quite mad

A typical insect it is
Having beautiful wing
With its compound eyes on head
It can see like a king

It pollinates several flowers
Both domestic and wild
Around the globe it occurs
Diminishing are their current number and kind

Its colour combination is very attractive and refreshing
One looks at it with wide eyes
And tries to take it in hand
Though with a great speed it flies.

4. The Cricket

I have the childhood memories
Of crickets chirping around
Breaking the silence of night
And stridulating in musical delight

Before I learnt playing cricket
And went to the cricket ground
Thanks to my grandparents
Who made me familiar with cricket's sound

House crickets are mostly harmless
Mole crickets destroy roots of plants
Both are nocturnal and omnivorous
Often feeding on insects like ants

Crickets love dark moist places to hide
Only the male does musical chirping
Long antennae act as a sensor
Hind legs help in instant jumping.

5. The Earthworm

Slimy, segmented, streamlined super worms
Earthworms are full of life
They wriggle, crawl, till and toil
To keep the soil alive

No eyes, nose, arms or feet
Yet they traverse the dirt with ease
Making the soil airy, porous and fertile
Respiring through moist skin, in own style

Come summer they all get buried
To enter aestivation sleep and hide
Come rains, they all appear for a while
And form 'worm-casts', rich in nutrient side

They all are mud-feeders
And also feed on live and dead organic matter
Soil and plants owe a lot to them
They are true macro-decomposer

If the worm has a bump (Clitellum)
It is sexually mature
And mucus comes out of clitellum
This also does reproductive chores

Male and female organs are borne in one
Yet they don't self-fertilize
Each cocoon on hatching produces one worm
A farmers' friend is thus born

The entire earth belongs to you
You are Gods' favourite creature
My dear earthworm!
You are not just a bait
You are both
A servant and a master.

6. The Honeybee

Honeybees may start early in the day
And follow the direction of the sun
Best properties in life
Knowing where to stop and when to run

There is division of labour in the colony
A worker is busy in collecting pollen
A drone is to mate with the only queen
The queen lays eggs having tapering abdomen

Dancing in circles
It tells of food close to the hive
And recognizes the odour
Of a flower on its way

Performs tail-wagging dance
For food at a distance
Working ceaselessly
During the whole day

In the honey crop
Nectar is converted into honey
It communicates in a language it knows
It can sting you
On disturbing a hive
It works very hard
Never begs or bows.

7. The Ladybird Beetle

What a designer beetle it is?
With seven black spots
On scarlet red
Feeding on aphids
And scale insects
You make the garden
Free of pests

Lady bird or Lady flies
As you are called
Throughout you command
An unparalleled respect

Your tiny black legs
And moving antennae
Make you favourite over the rest

Children consider you
Very lucky indeed
And crawl you on arms
For telling the fate
On your sweet will
You walk and walk
But suddenly you stop
And fly off the place

Your vibrant colours
Include orange and yellow
Your spots may vary
From few to twenty four or so

On kicking your body
A fluid comes out
To repel usual foes
Thin and transparent
Wings take you around the globe.

8. The Praying Mantis

Praying mantis rotates it head
Its forelegs working like hands
In catching insects it looks around
Showing its own ways and trends

Males use pheromones to locate a female
They are smaller brown
Females are large green
And lay about hundred eggs,

Which is often in an egg-case cemented to?
Or on a leaf hanging down
Two large grasping
Spiked forelegs
Make it an ideal
Predatory insect

An expert in camouflage
And concealment
Threat display includes
Wing fanning and hissing
Organic gardeners
Rear their eggs

Travelling in night
They avoid predators
Often photographed in a prayer like posture
Through bio-control, they eradicate pests
On crops of rice and sugar cane
A praying mantis rests.

9. The Mahseer

A man is filled with a great joy
When a mahseer strikes the rod
A mahseer being caught in net
Can be judged by a distant nod

From its large head
It derives its name
Unmatched is its meat
And unparalled its fame

In a golden mahseer
The head length is more
It dwells in rivers and streams
Hardly comes to shore

In a deep bodied mahseer
The head length is less
May live in lakes, perhaps
It is omnivorous in habits

Mahseer is an endangered fish
With scales and powerful tail
It is most easy to distinguish
Between male and a female

It may breed in rainy season
In shallow areas of a river
Sometime swimming against the current
It also performs water stunts

It is an attractive game fish
With great conservative value
Some states are protecting it
With scales shining golden-yellow.

10. The Frog

With a slimy skin
And pale green spots
Helped by large hind legs
A frog jumps from place to place

In rainy season
They come out in large number
When the male croaks loudly
To call his female partner

With a short blunt snout
And large protruding eyes
Its hump is especially conspicuous
When a frog is squatting

Insectivorous in habit
The frog has a sticky tongue
Its hind legs are a delicacy for some
And thus another frog succumbs

Being non-poisonous and harmless
They were sacrificed for dissections in labs
As their morphology was similar to man
But now, on their use, there is a ban

Of late, there is a decline
In their number and kind
I wish they continue to breed
Roaming freely and easy to find.

11. The Common Indian Toad

You should not be scared
When you find a toad
Jumping it enters your home
From a nearby road

A variety of toads occur
Common Indian toad
Appears quite ugly
Its foul smell really makes it unlovely

It is nocturnal in habit
And feeds on insects
Trapping them with the sticky tongue
During daytime often it rests

Having no teeth on either jaw
Their warts have poison glands
Behind each tympanum
Unpalatable secretion saves them from prey.

12. The Chameleon

The chameleon takes
The colour of its surroundings
With its eyes and head large
And a prehensile tail

It can dart away its body
With the help of its tail
Catching an insect
That may come on its way

It is famous for changing colour
Red, Brown, Green and Yellow it's favourite
Its claws are also
Meant for grasping tight

In grass and on road bushes
It may be seen
Always eager to catch prey
At dawn and dusk

It resembles a garden
Lizards in shape
A crest on head
Makes him great.

13. The Cobra

Cobra occurs where humans live
Unknowingly it may come
It has a wider distribution
Both in fields and near houses

Cobra is recognizable by its head
And pointed tail
There is a difference
Between male and female

Shields on its head
Are quite large, so are the ventral shields
Third supralabial scale
Touches the nostril and the eye

The tongue of a cobra is deeply forked
At the base of grooved fangs
Are poison glands
The skull and jaw bones are very flexible

When disturbed a cobra may strike
Fangs may serve as hypodermic needles
Injecting a neurotoxic poison
Which can cause death by
Paralysis of respiratory muscles

Cobra poison is very virulent
Affecting spinal cord and brain
Reduces coagulation of blood
And brings death by asphyxiation.

14. The Krait

The krait is a poisonous snake
Having mid-dorsal hexagonal scales
In a krait, the scale,
On the head and underneath are large
The fourth infra-labial is largest

As usual it has a bifid tongue
And poison glands
And strikes its victim
With great speed

It injects large quantity of poison
The victim feels unbearable abdominal pains
Due to haemolysis of erythrocytes
And paralysis of trunk and limbs

Krait usually runs
With a great speed
Only anti-venom of krait
May be used in hour of need.

15. The Pit Viper

Pit vipers are common in terai and hill
In a pit viper, the head
Scales are small
It has a loreal pit
Between eye and nostril

Loreal pits are an evolutionary way
To precisely feel the size and the heat of a prey
An opening of infra-red organs
They ensure snake's high-tech display

Their fangs are large and hinged
And remain folded
Against the roof of mouth
They can swallow large preys
Without any doubt

The venom of a pit viper
Is mainly haemotoxin
It destroys red blood cells
And harms the circulatory system

It is a mixture of enzymes
Designed to help the snake
To kill and digest its prey
Usually it does not bite, but it may

A red fluid oozes out
From wound with massive destruction
This sometime necessitates
Immediate amputation

In some worst cases
Death may result
Due to paralysis of vasomotor centres
And exhaustion results from profuse bleeding.

16. The Ghariyal

You live in deep pools of river
With feeble current
In water, you can make
Many a stunt

You live in water
Which is so deep
Artificial tears are "crocodile tears"
Although you hardly weep

Long is your snout
And jaws strong
You can swallow your prey
And commit no wrong

You have an inverted pitcher ('ghara') on your head
That gives you the name
As a fish-eater
You have excellent fame

A female Ghariyal lays
Enough eggs in the sand
On hatching, they make a croaking sound
And call for mother
Who takes the hatchlings
To the water of river

Man kills you for your skin
To make clothes and other things
You love to eat fish with no noise
And swim without losing your poise

The project crocodile
Does not allow your number to decline
May you always live in Ganges water
And there always shine.

17. The Olive Ridley Turtle

Olive Ridley, Olive Ridley
Who gave you this name
I am sure the heart shaped Olive Carapace
Brought you the name and fame..!

Smallest of the sea turtles
You prefer open pelagic waters
Love solitary life and roam around
Until the mating season arrives

'Arribada' is synchronized
Group nesting and mating in masses
When they use sea-winds and tide
To reach Rookery beaches

A female lays about hundred eggs in batches
Nesting in India lasts from June to December
'Gahirmatha' in Orrisa is on world map
To watch them laying eggs in large number

They forage on jelly fish, crab and shrimp
Occasionally algae and seaweed they eat
Once most abundant of all sea turtles
They are poached for leather, eggs and meat

Egg laden females
Lumber on the shores
It's when they are caught
By fishermen and many more

Olive Ridley of world fame
Can't retract their head
They are trapped as flippers get choked
In the small mesh of gill nets

Let us save Olive Ridley
From becoming extinct
For they are attractive creatures
With a lovely carapace, so utterly distinct.

18. The Great Indian Bustard

A native of Gujarat and Rajasthan
It occurs in semi-arid- deserts
It's a majestic bird with a black band
Running across its breast

It stands a metre tall
With dorsal side brown
It's under parts are white
And a black cap on the head

Omnivorous in habit
It feeds early in the morning
Resting in grass during the day
In mating season
The male dances like a peacock
Attracting females of the harem

A single egg is laid
And incubated for over a fortnight
After hatching out of the egg
Hatchlings can walk straight in delight

The bird is conserved
In desert sanctuary of Rajasthan
To our satisfaction
Their number is increasing as per plan.

19. The Great Indian Hornbill

It is one of the rarest bird species
And has been adopted in the logo of Bombay Natural History
Society
The helmeted bird has a beautiful colour combination
It is one of the emblematic birds of our nation

It has a red beak
With a massive yellow and black tail
Female is smaller in size
Than the normal male

It is a good omen to see a Hornbill
'Dhanesh' it is called
In all its variants in the country
Its plumage is very colourful

A native of heavy forests
Of Tarai and Western Ghats
The bird often makes nest holes
In Banyan and Peepal trees
Predominantly frugivorous
State bird of Kerala and Arunachal Pradesh
Long lived bird may live for fifty years.

20. The Himalayan Monal

State bird of Uttarakhand
The Himalayan Monal has a crest
It dwells in alpine oak forests
And makes no nest

Nine colours it has
Danphe they call it in Nepal
It's their national bird
It's famous as Himalayan Monal

How royal it looks
With colours so bright
Purple, red, green, blue and yellow
Alpine forests too, truly love this fellow

So common it was
In ancient days
Men have reduced them
In many a ways

It is poached for crest
A symbol of man's pride on cap
The poor bird has no means to defend it
Falling to human's ugly design and rack.

21. The House Crow

Black beauty amongst the Indian bird
Your voice is very harsh
"Nothing escapes them", wrote Mark Twain
Cunning and agile you stay undeterred

An old belief goes, if on the high parapet
A crow speaks loud, taking a long flight,
An uninformed guest is likely to arrive by the evening
Enough to churn emotions right

Although omnivorous in habit
They may eat anything they find
When hungry, they may snatch away from children
Any object or eatable of any kind

The story goes that a crow had snatched
Bread and butter from Lord Krishna with tact
And in return, the lord immortalized him
For doing this innocent act

Although no one likes them
For their looks and harsh voice
Religious beliefs have saved them
And their purposeful strive

Truly wild, house crows act as
Efficient municipal scavenger
To anyone in India
They are no stranger..!

22. The House Sparrow (Gauraiyya)

As the most commonly seen bird
Gauraiyya occurs throughout the country
Freely moving and nesting
In the house meant for us

With dull brown colour
Sexual dimorphism is distinct
Adapted for perching
Are their feet

Three to five white greyish eggs
Are laid by female
They hatch soon
And cry for food and help

Sparrows are omnivorous
Anything they can consume
They can come very near to man
If no harm is done to them

Their beak is small
Any eyes sharp
Without fear they grab grain
From our courtyard and hop

Their number has declined
As we have fallen trees
Greenery we have destroyed
In life, we don't imagine price of these.

23. The Kite (Cheel)

The kite is a large bird
Flying very high in the sky
Singly or a few of them
May rise quite high

Its plumage is brown
It has a forked tail
Elongated toed are for grasping
With a sharp beak in male or female

It is carnivorous in habit
And largely a scavenger
Hides in green vegetation
Roams in sky as a messenger

A friend of the farmer
It kills rodents and reptiles
It can go in the sky
For miles and miles…

Very powerful it is
Like an eagle
Its eyes are very sharp
Keeping constant vigil.

24. The Neelkanth
(The Blue Jay)

It is a good omen
To see a Neelkanth on journcy
Where you may gain
Reputation and money

Widely distributed the bird
Has a beautiful plumage
Its appearance reminds
Of Lord Shiva's image

When the sea was churned
Among other things
Poison was also there
Lord Shiva consumed it

And through his divine power
Stopped poison in his neck
Which became blue
Hence 'Neelkanth' is a synonym of Shiva

The bird is also known
For its wisdom and cleverness
It is a common saying
That in some past birth
It was a 'patwari'*
And had not done
Justice to village folk
Hence they cursed the bird
And it had to take poison
But Shiva made it beautiful bird
Anyway, it is a pleasure
To see the bird hunting in streams on the way
Especially when you are on a train journey
And the fields are passing away.

*patwari: Registrar of a villages land account

25. The Sarus Crane

Tallest of all the cranes
As tall as a man
An iconic bird of open wetlands
It actually was in the run
For the India's
National Bird Position
An elegant crane
Painted for its looks
With about eight feet wing span
Weighing seven kilos
Forage on tubers and insects
Body grey bill long and red legs

Within their territories
They do loud trumpeting
And dance-like movements
One of India's resident birds
They breed in monsoon
One or two eggs are incubated by them
A symbol of marital fidelity
Sarus cranes pair for life

Chicks thus born
Are yellowish brown
And follow their parents
In a couple of days
They are wiped out
In many a ways
What a befitting title?
It's 'State bird of Uttar Pradesh'.

26. The Koyal
(The Black Cuckoo)

Hopping among the mango trees
You sing a melodious song
So sweet is your voice
I can listen you for the day long

You are a small bird
With black colour and attractive eyes
Only you can show mirror to lookism
With your inner beauty, melody and a poise

Who knows you may sing for your own brother
Who may be sitting; may be on the next branch
You call him again and again
Though quite unable to see him there

People call you very wise and clever
As you put your eggs in the Crow's nest
Until they hatch you are quite free
In beautiful shadow you do take rest

You sang when I was young
In autumn with a pitch so high
You sing when I am old
And these seasons make me sigh..!

27. The Owl

Living in dark places
And holes in the trees
An owl enjoys a wider distribution
It is nocturnal in habit

A carnivorous bird
Feeding on reptiles and rodents
It is of great value
To the agriculturist

As a vehicle of Goddess Lakshmi
The owl is considered very intelligent
An animal with a plumage brown and grey
And lighter under parts, with feathery legs

With large rounded and
Forwardly directing eyes
And two prominent feather tufts
Above head, look like ears

The eyes are so fearful
And so is its call
During night it is deadly on rats
Can scare you even at a mall

The speaking of an owl
Is harsh with no grace
It is sometimes considered an ill omen
A man has to face

In our mythology
An owl has a high place
Its looks though may be ugly
And it may not have grace.

28. The Parrot

Noisiest of all Indian birds
Their squawking call is unique
Great at talking and intelligent in learning
They are famous as pet species

In male Indian rose-ringed parakeet
They bear red rings around neck
Red beaks and red circles around eyes
Add beauty to its perfect poise

Indian ringnecks are native
To Asia and Africa
They seem to have overcome
Urbanisation and deforestation

Pairing is done during early winter
From April to June they care for the young
Fledglings leave the nest
Before the monsoon

The have been named
After the famous Austrian naturalist Kramer
Adapted to live in disturbed habitats
Chicks often dwell in tree holes

Distinctly dark green in colour
With attractive red beaks
They have since years
Been trapped as pet species.

29. The Peacock

A sight of a dancing
Male peacock is a joy
For colourful feathers it has
And screams as 'mee-awe"

Aptly called our National bird
Their call is loud
Neck is bright green
Metallic sheen, we are proud

Omnivorous in habit
On anything they subsist
Calling for rain Gods
During July and August

Well marked sexual dimorphism
Is displayed by the pheasant
Their feet are adapted for running
And this is on record

The female has a short tail
A keen sense of hearing and vision
It is vigilant throughout
When you approach her, with or without a mission

Reduction in forest cover
Poaching for eggs, crest, feathers and meat
Is a reason for their decline
Pesticides in fields
Also take a heavy toll
In the current time.

30. The Pigeon

They body of a pigeon
Is very neat
It has feathers strong
And scales on feet

It likes food grains
Offered by man
And may drink water
From any utensil or pan

Its flight muscles are
Red and strong
And can fly
A long distance

A trained pigeon is
An asset to its master
It is considered wise
As a faithful messenger

The blue rock pigeon
Is a common variety
They live in human settlements
Although white pet pigeons
Are also rarely seen
And valued as
Great symbol of world peace

The male pigeon dances
And twists its neck
To attract a female of its choice
It gently touches female's neck
To whom it is always nice
Often they make a characteristic sound
With a "guttergoon"
This echoes all around

In older times
They used to carry
A message or a letter
Both in war and peace
In a way
Much better than today
Now they hardly
Carry a post unless trained
To these duties
They hardly attend.

31. The Vulture

This huge bird measures
Several feet across the wings
It has a black or smoky colour
And two white patches on the thighs

The commonest Indian vulture
Has a white band extending
Nearly the whole lengths
Of each wing on the underside

They collect in large gatherings
To demolish animal carcasses
With astonishing promptness
And incredible speed

They come automatically, in hour of our need
Adapted for perching
And eyes keen on searching
Strong are their feet

Occurring throught the country
They like blunt trees and barren lands
Strongly carnivorous and famous scavengers
Facing a toll of Diclofenac and showing decreasing trends

Their number has declined
Due to pesticide use
They have been immortalized
In literature and muse.

32. The Weaver Bird (Baya)

How ingenious you are
In weaving your nest
Until you complete,
Take no rest

Elaborately woven, a nest has a bottle like shape
Where your eggs and embryos rest
They hatch even without opening their eyes
With a body without feathers and jest

When you go out
On a food collecting trip
Little grain you bring
For your small ones
You put the grain in their red mouth
With no teeth found
And they make a chirping sound
This can be heard all around

Your nest is built on hanging twigs
So that no creature can approach it
Sometimes the nest has a partition
The modern architecture can't match it

Denudation of forest cover
Is responsible for your decline
Please weave a nest for me
Which I can call mine..!

Your love for children
Is apparent in your eyes
A strong sense of territory you have
Your behaviour is really wise..!

So hard you work, that man can't imagine
Bringing straw for the nest
You really look strong and genuine
No doubt 'Baya' *you* are the best..!

33. The Woodpecker (Kathphorwa)

Woodpeckers are now rarely seen
Since we destroyed tree trunks and green
Earlier they occurred throughout the wooded country
In orchards and grooves around
And gardens which are sultry

Their bill is strong
For making a hole in the tree
They dig into rotten wood
For insects, this is a reality

They have a long protractible tongue
And cling on to the trees
Bright in colour and a beak as a masterpiece
I always get attracted to these.

34. The Barasinga

Barasinga occurs in swampy areas
At many places
Slightly smaller in size
Than a Sāmbhar, it is

The barasinga is a deer species
With twelve antlers
Its head and antlers
Are kept in drawing rooms as trophies

The poor animal falls prey for its looks, skin and leather
They have a strong sense of smell
When alarmed the herd disappears quickly
After giving a sharp call

They graze in late morning and evening
During the day, take rest
Antlers are also turned into ash
Used in curing ailments of Chest

They are killed for antlers
And meat, which is palatable
As a threatened species
Their conservation is desirable.

35. The Bat

A bat is the true flying mammal
And can compete very well with birds
Normally the pinna is large
And tail long in an insect-eating bat
While the fruit-eating bat
Has a large body, with a
Small pinna and no tail
A proverb says
That in bat's house
Even the guest will have
To hang upside down
As they all do it, always
In every location
Bat's forearms are modified into a wing
Hind legs are with sharp curved claws
Keeping Bat's head down when it is sleeping
Hook like teeth of the young bat
Help it firmly grip the maternal teats
While the mother is flying during the night
In a bat, fingers support
The wing-web like ribs
They open and close the patagium
Keeping it taut when expanded
Bats rely on echo-location
For catching their prey
In flight bats keep their mouth open
And emit supersonic sounds
Engineers and architects have to learn
Many a thing from bat
Their aerodynamics is remarkable
That nobody can match.

36. The Blackbuck

Second only to the Cheetah
This antelope is fastest on four legs
A native of Asia
Once it roamed entire Indian Sub-Continent

Diurnal and gregarious in habit
They live in a herd of around 5-50
Their V-shaped spiralling horns
Sweeping backwards look majestic

Dark brown to black
Is the upper coat of male
This species has a narrow muzzle
And a short tail

Female lacks horn
And is light in colour
Bishnois of Rajasthan protect them
With a great valour

Their life span
Is about ~ fifteen years in wild
Underside of their belly
Is often pale white

Male undertakes lekking drive
To attract a female of choice
Hunting this antelope is strictly forbidden
Under laws of Indian Wildlife.

37. The Camel

Camel- o- Camel
You are a large animal
So well adapted to desert life
O 'Ship of the desert' how much you strive

Your eyes are small
And neck so long
Legs are stout
And body so strong

Every part of your body
Shows physiological adaptation
To live in the desert is no joke
It can go without water long and not just a mock

Eye lashes protect
Its eyes from sand
One or two humps that fad
Serve as source of reserve so grand

The colour itself suits desert life
A high body temperature
Is maintained by it to conserve water throughout
In peace and strife

Feeds on desert bushes and trees
And provides transport, flesh, hide and the wool
Very intelligent it really is
No one should see it as innocent or fool.

38. The Elephant

In India, You are part of
Tradition and culture
You are indeed a wonder animal
And so are your looks n posture

You are worshipped in
Every Indian home;
How intelligent you are
With body like a dome

The 'Tilak' on your head
Takes us with surprise;
You have a keen sense of hearing
And quite handsome and wise

Your trunk is a remarkable organ
Your large ears appear as fan
The giant size and small eyes
Also make children your fan

It is no wonder
That 'Ganesha' has taken your shape
Your short tail is simply beautiful
Excellent is your gait

Vegetarian you are; yet so powerful
What a majestic is really your sight
To and fro and side to side
Lucky are the guys who get your ride.

39. The Gangetic Dolphin

Sharing its habitat
With crocodiles and freshwater turtles
The Gangetic Dolphin is an aquatic mammal
It's the 'National Aquatic Animal of India'

It resides in deep pools in the Ganga
And Brahmaputra river systems
Because of the sound it produces in breathing
The animal is called 'Susu'

Its colour is greyish-brown
Although the young ones are dark in colour
It is poached for meat and oil
And to defend itself, has no armour

They prefer fish as food
And swallow their prey
Pollution and habitat loss
Are the main reasons of their decay

As their eyes lack a lens
They are also termed 'blind'
Female are larger than male
Poaching, pollution and fertilizers are taking a toll abound

The female rears the young
Spending whole life in water
Alarmingly few in number
They need our protection cover.

40. The Otter

India is home to
Three of the thirteen species of otters
Primarily aquatic and crepuscular
Aptly termed as "wetland ambassadors"

Principal predators of aquatic environs
Love rocky stretches to rest and den
Extremely versatile, shy and elusive
Hunt in groups on banks with vegetation

A family has dad, mother and pups
Lead a nomadic life between March and August
Settling in winter to breed and rear pups
Communicate using wails, whistles and chirps

They suddenly dive
And grasp the fish with snout
Common and small clawed otters reside in the Himalayas
Smooth coat otter is distributed throughout

Feeding range could be twelve kilometres or more
They are intelligent and playful, difficult to ignore
They have round head, vibrissae on face
Tail is flattened, and webbed feet have strong claws

They are at a risk
And killed for pelt and fur
Still not much is known
About this wonderful creature

Scent glands are used for marking the objects
Mainly a fish-eater, they love cat-fish and snakehead..!
They dwell in streams, seasonal swamps and wetland
But they are equally comfortable on land.

41. The Gir Lion

Four of you, standing back to back
Adore our National Emblem
An apt symbol of courage and beauty
You indeed carry a Lion's heart

Gifted with golden yellow hair
And body strong and stout
The Sasan Gir in Gujarat is your natural home
On this no one should have a little doubt

The male lion has a mane
The female is slim and daring
She feeds her cubs
And is very caring

A lion guards its territory
To hunt and mate
So that cubs can trot freely
And learn life's trait

They live in a group
We know as 'pride'
Poachers often target them
For body parts and hide

A lion becomes young
At the age of four
And produces,
The familiar Lion's roar

Nilgai, Wild boar and Barasinga
Are its favourite feast
Thank you God, thanks again
For giving us this beast..!

42. The Himalayan Black Beer

The Himalayan black bear's coat is shaggy
Muzzle long and brown
Its eyes are very small
And ears round

The Himalayan black bear dwells in
Broad leaved and Coniferous forests
Preferring steep forested hills
Passing long time in winter-sleep

It is diurnal and solitary, lies idle in daytime
Reclining in rock-crevices
And tree-hollows
Is its favourite pastime

Cheerfully it stands on hind legs
To look for distant object
When its crescent on the chest
Is seen at its best
Three year male is an adult
They usually mate in October
One or two cubs are born in winter
And the offspring stay with the mother

The beer loves to climb
Trees with honey comb or termite
Sharp curved claws hold large body
Against the tree trunk firm and tight

Their hearing sensitivity is twice of humans
And twenty five years of life span
Body parts are used in traditional medicine
Poaching and habitat loss are two main reasons of their decline.

43. The Hangul
(The Kashmir Stag)

Hangul is a majestic deer
Dearly called Kashmir-Stag
Dachigam is its last bastion
It's a relative of Red-deer

Hangul is famous for changing its coat
And the antlers may have up to sixteen points
Life span is about eighteen years
Each antler has five lines

Loud roar of the male sounds like a leopard
And rutting starts in September
Fawn are born in May or June
Within three years they are mature

They inhabit mountain, high-valleys
And dense riverine forests
Dwindling in numbers, they are at risk
From human interference and depleting forests.

44. The Hanuman Langur

A Hanuman Langur
Enough power it wields in tail
If you kill a hanuman langur
You may land in the Jail

Native of North India, vegetarian they are
So powerful to chase
Their colour silvery-grey
With a black face

They live in forest trees
Jumping from one tree to another
Depend on tree nuts
Which they consume together

They live in a small group
Of three to four
Many a thing about their behaviour
We have to learn more

As a threatened species
They are liked by many
Intelligent enough and considered sacred
They dwell on tree's canopy.

45. The Indian Rhinoceros

The massive beast is a mega herbivore
And loves alluvial grasslands and forests
Its black horn is pure keratin
Which starts to show after six years

The horn is present on adult male and female
And not on the young
They may mate round the year
And show no specific calving season

Indian Rhino is larger than Javan
Second in size to Indian Elephant
They congregate in hot noon to socialize
Making wallow a worth seeing event

Wallowing helps in heat-regulation
And keeps the flies at bay
Mud coating keeps skin cool
And ectoparasites away

They use ten different sounds
And dung heaps as communication points
They defecate in communal latrines
Segmented hide has armoured lines

These grazers are excellent swimmers
With keen sense of hearing and smell
Rhino horn is highly prized
And a reason for their down fall

A female matures early than a male
A sixty centimetre horn has three kilo weight
They have about sixteen month's gestation
A calf is around sixty kilo in weight

Rhino is State animal of Assam
Its horn is used in Asian medicine
Rhino is pride of Indian wildlife
It needs an all-round protection.

46. The Indian Tiger

Oh my dear beast
You appear from the east
You roar on the mountain
Like a flowing fountain

The Project Tiger has saved you
From further decline
How majestic you are?
That you always shine

The Project is currently run
In forty eight tiger reserves
The country has paid enough attention
That it truly deserves

You are the National Animal
Of my country
Your looks are divine
And so is your wild entry

Many of your body parts have medicinal value
For which you face death
Such a charismatic beast falls
To the vicious plan of organized poacher's trap

Your stripes are simply beautiful
And breath-taking
To see you again in wild
I have a craving.

47. The Mongoose (Nevla)

With a small snout
And a bushy tapering tail
This slender carnivore can stand on belly
To give an alarming call so loud

Occurring in a field
It feeds on mice
Hence for a farmer
It is always nice

No fear of a snake
When a mongoose is there
Now it has become
Threatened and rare

It can fight well with a snake
Attacking him in the neck
When its shining incisors penetrate
Piercing the neck without a mistake

Sometimes it destroys the crop
Digging a burrow to live
Taking very little for itself
More, though it may give

Organized poaching is bent upon
To wipe out this beautiful carnivore
It's hair and skin are in great demand
Making it popular in wildlife trade and folklore..!

48. The Monkey

Monkeys are a menace at places
But their numbers have declined
Highly adapted to live in disturbed habitats
They feed anything and don't just mind

In groups they live
And jump from branch to branch
Female carrying a young on back
Not hesitating on human stance

Slowly they come
And may beg for food
Often they frighten you
You can't judge their mood

Their frivolous nature
Is so well known
Often they ape you
For reasons unknown

Empty threat is
Famous, among all
Monkey's friendship
Fickle friendship they call

They were earlier used to study
The effects of drugs and cosmetics
Social mammals they are and they love to hug
And find each other's lice with patience and tactics.

49. The Nilgai

Nilgais live in open fields
They often dwell in herds
They are powerful burly beasts
Which often become active after dusk

They eat crops
And may attack men
They just don't fear
Whatever the reason

Well-built they are
With bodies strong
Keen sense of hearing they have
As you come along

They are killed
For their palatable meat
Though killing a Nilgai
Is a cognizable offence.

50. The Red Panda

Distantly related to the Giant Panda of China
Larger than a cat, with a ringed tail like a Racoon
Apparently a cross between the above three
Charismatic indeed they are

Active at dawn and dusk; solitary and shy during the day
They live in understory of bamboo and hollow trees
Their pelage is reddish-orange brown
And feed on bird eggs and bees

On hot days they sleep loose with legs dangling down
When the chilly winds on a mountain abound
They curl and the tail becomes
A face-wrap around

Both sexes are alike, with unique 'tear drops'
North-Eastern Himalayas in India are their native range
Where they are seen
As key indicators of Forest-change

State animal of Sikkim; sometimes called as Cat-beer
They petrol their territories and mark it with urine
They often lick their front paws and rub their back like a cat
Habitat fragmentation and climate change seems their
immediate threat.

51. The Indian Pangolin (Scaly Ant Eater)

Indian pangolin can climb trees
An old mammal, it can curve its body into a ball
It leads a solitary life
During night it can stroll n stroll

Body is covered with armoured scales
Made of keratin like our nails
Tongue is a long sticky organ
They have wonderful prehensile tails

They lack teeth and ability to chew
And feed on termite and ants
Lack scale on snout, eyes and ears
They are famous as Scaly Ant Eaters

One-third of their body weight comes from scales
A male is often larger than female
And gestation period is
Around seventy five days

Mother nurses the young for three-four months
And moves them on its tail
At two years of age they are mature
But throughout the life grows its scale

Their insatiable appetite for insects
Gives them a wonderful role
They inhabit terrestrial ecosystem
Where they do Pest Control..!

52. The Thamin
(Brow-Antler Deer)

Endemic to Manipur, the Sangai
Dwells on floating algal mats
'Phumdi' forms a unique habitat
On which the Dancing deer rests

Sangai is a shy, gentle deer
Feeds in early morning hours
It is the State animal of Manipur
With a short life span of ~ten years

Rutting starts in early spring
When the male competes for a harem of females
A calf is born, after a gestation
Of around eight months

A popular folk-lore of Manipur shows
Sangai as a binding soul between human and nature
Truly, in protecting Sangai
We protect comely nature..!

The Keibul Lamjao is a National Park now
And a natural home to Sangai
Their small number is a cause of worry
Conservation and awareness we should apply.